A HOLIDAY GIFT FOR

Christy

FROM

with Love, Mom

CHRISTMAS IS...

CHRISTMAS IS GIVING

THEREFORE THE LORD HIMSELF WILL give you a sign: The virgin will be with child and will give birth to a son, and will call him Immanuel.

—ISAIAH 7:14

She will give birth to a son, and you are to give him the name Jesus, because he will save his people from their sins.

—MATTHEW 1:21

This is Christmas—the real meaning of it.

God loving, searching, giving Himself—to us.

Man's needing, receiving, giving himself—to God.

Redemption's glorious exchange of gifts!

Without which we cannot live;

Without which we cannot give to those we love
anything of lasting value.

This is the meaning of Christmas—
the wonder and the glory of it.

—RUTH BELL GRAHAM

The best Christmas gift of all

is the presence of a happy family

all wrapped up with one another.

What can I give Him,
Poor as I am?
If I were a shepherd,
I would bring a lamb,
If I were a Wise Man,
I would do my part—
Yet what I can I give Him,
Give my heart.

—CHRISTINA GEORGINA ROSSETTI

The greatest good of every giving is—
when the giver is in the gift.

—GEORGE MACDONALD

The Legend of the Poinsettia

A Mexican legend tells of a poor little girl who had no gift to give the Christ Child at the Christmas Eve service in their church. Watching others bring their gifts, her heart was filled with sadness until a strange visitor, perhaps an angel, told her than even the most humble gift, if it is given is love, is an excellent gift. The poor child gathered some green weeds and laid them by the manger. Suddenly, the bouquet of weeds burst into blooms of brilliant red in what was believed to be a Christmas miracle.

From that time on, the green leaves of the poinsettia turn bright red every year during the Christmas season as a gift to the Son of God.

It is not the gift, but the thought that counts.
—VAN DYKE

The way you spend Christmas is far more important than how much.

—HENRY DAVID THOREAU

CHRISTMAS IS MUSIC

———— ❋ ————

SUDDENLY A GREAT COMPANY OF THE
heavenly host appeared with the angel, praising
God and saying, "Glory to God in the highest, and
on earth peace to men on whom his favor rests."

—LUKE 2:13–14

Away in a Manger

Away in a manger, no crib for a bed,
The little Lord Jesus laid down His sweet head;
The stars in the sky looked down where He lay,
The little Lord Jesus, asleep on the hay.

The cattle are lowing; the Baby awakes,
But little Lord Jesus, no crying He makes;
I love Thee, Lord Jesus! Look down from the sky,
And stay by my cradle till morning is nigh.

Be near me, Lord Jesus, I ask Thee to stay
Close by me forever, and love me, I pray;
Bless all the dear children in Thy tender care,

And fit us for heaven, to live with Thee there.

—ATTRIBUTED TO MARTIN LUTHER

Silent Night

"Silent Night" was written in 1818 by an Austrian priest named Joseph Mohr. He was told the day before Christmas that the church organ was broken and would not be repaired in time for Christmas Eve. He was saddened by this and could not imagine Christmas without music. Deciding to compose a carol that could be sung by the choir to guitar music, he sat down and immediately wrote three stanzas. Later that night, the people in the little Austrian Church sang "Stille Nact" for the first time.

Silent night! Holy Night!
All is calm, all is bright
'Round yon virgin mother and Child,
Holy Infant, so tender and mild
Sleep in heavenly peace,
Sleep in heavenly peace.

The First Noel

The first noel the angel did say
Was to certain poor shepherds in fields as they lay;
In fields where they lay keeping their sheep
On a cold winter's night that was so deep.

They looked up and saw a star
Shining in the east, beyond them far;
And to the earth, it gave great light,
And so it continued both day and night.

And by the light of that same star,
Three wise men came from country far;
To seek for a king was their intent,
And to follow the star wherever it went.

Then entered in those wise men three,
Fall reverently upon their knee,
And offered there, in His presence,
Their gold and myrrh and frankincense.

Then let us all with one accord
Sing praises to our heavenly Lord,
That hath made heaven and earth of naught,
And with His blood mankind hath bought.

Noel, noel! Noel, noel!
Born is the King of Israel.

Hark! The Herald Angels Sing

Hark! The herald angels sing, "Glory to the newborn King;
Peace on earth, and mercy mild—God and sinners reconciled!"
Joyful, all ye nations rise, join the triumph of the skies;
With angelic hosts proclaim, "Christ is born in Bethlehem!"
Hark! The herald angels sing, "Glory to the newborn King!"

Christ, by highest heaven adored, Christ, the everlasting Lord!
Late in time behold Him come, offspring of a virgin's womb.
Veiled in flesh the Godhead see; hail the incarnate Deity,
Pleased as man with men to dwell, Jesus, our Emmanuel.
Hark! The herald angels sing, "Glory to the newborn King!"

Hail the heaven born Prince of Peace! Hail the Sun of Righteousness!
Light and life to all He brings, risen with healing in His wings.
Mild He lays His glory by, born that man no more may die,
Born to raise the sons of earth, Born to give them second birth.

Hark! The herald angels sing, "Glory to the newborn King!"

—JOHN WESLEY

Emmanuel

O come, O come, Emmanuel,
And ransom captive Israel,
That mourns in lonely exile here
Until the Son of God appear.

O come, Thou Dayspring, come and cheer
Our spirits by Thine advent here;
O drive away the shades of night

And pierce the clouds and bring us light.
Rejoice!
Rejoice!
Emmanuel shall come to thee,
O Israel.

O Come, All Ye Faithful

O come, all ye faithful, joyful and triumphant;
O come ye, O come ye to Bethlehem;
Come and behold Him; born the King of angels!
Refrain: O come, let us adore Him, Christ the Lord.

Sing, choirs of angels, sing in exultation,
O sing, all ye bright hosts of heav'n above!
Glory to God, all glory in the highest!
Refrain: O come, let us adore Him, Christ the Lord.

Yea, Lord, we greet Thee, born this happy morning,
Jesus, to Thee be all glory giv'n;
Word of the Father, now in flesh appearing!
Refrain: O come, let us adore Him, Christ the Lord.

—LATIN HYMN,
ENGLISH TRANSLATION BY FREDERICK OAKLEY

CHRISTMAS
IS TRADITION

❋

CHRISTMAS IS CELEBRATED ACROSS THE
world with a rich array of traditions. The practice of
singing Christmas carols appears to be almost as old as
the celebration of the day itself. In the first days of the
church, the bishops sang carols on Christmas Day, recalling
the songs sung by the angels at the birth of Christ. In
medieval times, the bells were tolled one hour before
midnight on Christmas Eve, giving the powers of
darkness notice of the approaching birth of the Savior.

Christmas plays and pageants are popular in Poland, where
the Christmas story is recited in verse and acted out by
marionettes. In some parts of South America as the
Nativity is reenacted, an Indian lullaby is sung to quiet
the Christ child in His cradle of straw. In India, decorated
mango and banana trees replace the more traditional
evergreens. In Hawaii, Christmas starts with the coming
of the Christmas Tree Ship, bringing a great load of
Christmas fare. Santa Claus also arrives by boat.

Did You Know?

Saint Nicholas was a fourth-century bishop of Myra, located in what is now called Turkey. He was the patron saint of children, as well as sailors, because he would secretly deliver money or presents to the poor and also was credited with calming the raging sea.

History of the Christmas Tree

The Christmas tree originated in Germany in the sixteenth century. It was common for the German people to decorate fir trees, both inside and out, with roses, apples, and colored paper. It is believed that Martin Luther, the Protestant reformer, was the first to light a Christmas tree with candles. While coming home one dark winter's night near Christmas, Luther was struck with the beauty of the starlight shining through the branches of a small fir tree outside his home. He duplicated the starlight by using candles attached to the branches of his indoor Christmas tree.

Christmas in Norway

The Nordic tradition of burning a yule log dates back to medieval times. Originally, an entire tree was carefully chosen and brought into the house with great ceremony. The large end of the tree would be placed into the fireplace, while the rest of it stuck out into the room. The yule log would be lit from the remains of the previous year's log, which had been stored away for the occasion, and it would be fed slowly into the fire through the twelve days of Christmas.

Christmas in Russia

Even though Christmas was first introduced into Russia more than a thousand years ago when Great Duke Vladimir of the Russian Royal family converted to Christianity, it was not until the early eighteenth century that the celebration was Westernized. Czar Peter the Great introduced a great many Western European practices, including the traditional evergreen Christmas tree, which was decorated with apples, candy, nuts, and candles.

History of the Candy Cane

In the late 1800s, a candy maker in Indiana wanted to express the meaning of Christmas through a symbol made of candy. He came up with the idea of bending one of his white candy sticks into the shape of a cane and incorporating several symbols of Christ's love and sacrifice. First, he used a plain white peppermint stick. The color white symbolizes the purity and sinless nature of Jesus.

Next, he added three small stripes to symbolize the pain inflicted upon Jesus before His death on the cross. He added a bold stripe to represent the blood Jesus shed for humanity. When looked at with the crook on top, it looks like a shepherd's staff, because Jesus is the Shepherd of man. If you turn it upside down, it becomes the letter "J," symbolizing the first letter in Jesus' name. The candy cane serves as a lasting reminder of what Christmas is really all about.

Light Up the World

In the early 1900s a young Denver boy who was sick asked his father to put lights on the big evergreen just outside his window. The boy's father, who operated an electrical business, strung colored lights on the evergreen. His son watched them sparkle like emeralds and rubies against their white mantle of snow.

In horse-drawn carriages and chugging automobiles, people came for miles around to admire the tree. The next year, neighbors joined in the outdoor tree-trimming.

It wasn't long before the lighted Christmas trees spread from home to home and became a holiday tradition. Today, in city parks, along highways, on dark and snow-drifted lawns alike, lighted living trees remind millions of the birth of Christ.

—GRADY JOHNSON

CHRISTMAS IS CHILDREN

❋

THE WAY TO CHRISTMAS LIES THROUGH
an ancient gate.... It is a little gate, child-high,
child-wide, and there is a password: "Peace on
earth to men of good will." May you, this
Christmas, become as a little child again and
enter into His kingdom.

—ANGELO PATRI

None will ever find a way

To banish Christ from Christmas Day...

For with each child there's born again

A mystery that baffles men.

—HELEN STEINER RICE

Welcome to you, sweet Christmas Eve,

says the heart of every child.

The smell of hot cider,

the kindling of the fire,

the warmth of wool mittens,

the sounds of merry laughter

and singing of the carols

fill the night with a song

never to be forgotten.

—LANCE WUBBELS

The joy of brightening a child's heart creates the magic of Christmas.

—W. C. JONES

Children's Wishes

In the United Kingdom, children write their requests in letters to Father Christmas, but instead of dropping them into the mailbox, they toss them into the fireplace. According to legend, the draft carries the letters up the chimney, and Father Christmas reads the smoke.

When the younger children wake early on Christmas morning, they find stockings at the ends of their beds and a few presents on the floor. Later, the whole family gathers around the lighted tree to open the rest of the presents.

You can never truly enjoy Christmas

until you can look up into the Father's face

and tell Him you have received His Christmas gift.

—JOHN R. RICE

CHRISTMAS IS HOPE & LOVE

For to us a child is born, to us a son is
given, and the government will be on
his shoulders. And he will be called
Wonderful Counselor, Mighty God,
Everlasting Father, Prince of Peace.
Of the increase of his government and
peace there will be no end. He will reign
on David's throne and over his kingdom,
establishing and upholding it with justice
and righteousness from that time on
and forever. The zeal of the Lord
Almighty will accomplish this.

—ISAIAH 9:6–7

In a world that seems not only to be changing, but even to be dissolving, there are some tens of millions of us who want Christmas to be the same…with the same old greeting "Merry Christmas" and no other.

We long for the abiding love among men of goodwill which the season brings… believing in this ancient miracle of Christmas with its softening, sweetening influence to tug at our heartstrings once again.

We want to hold on to our old customs and traditions because they strengthen our family ties, bind us to our friends, make us one with all mankind for whom the child was born, and bring us back again to the God who gave His only begotten Son, that "whosoever believeth in Him should not perish, but have everlasting life."

So we will not "spend" Christmas…nor "observe" Christmas.

We will "keep" Christmas—keep it as it is…in all the loveliness of its ancient traditions.

May we keep it in our hearts, that we may be kept in its hope.

—PETER MARSHALL

I am not alone at all, I thought.

I was never alone at all.

And that, of course, is the message of Christmas.

We are never alone.

Not when the night is darkest, the wind coldest,

the world seemingly most indifferent.

For this is still the time God chooses.

—TAYLOR CALDWELL

I have always thought of Christmas…as a good time:
a kind, forgiving, charitable, pleasant time;
the only time I know of, in the long calendar of the year,
when men and women seem by one consent
to open their shut-up hearts freely….

And though it has never put
a scrap of gold or silver in my pocket,
I believe that it has done me good,
and will do me good.

And so, as Tiny Tim said,
"A merry Christmas to us all;
God bless us, every one!"

—CHARLES DICKENS

Here is love,

that God sent His Son,

His Son who never offended,

His Son who was always

His delight.

—JOHN BUNYAN

Loving Father, help us remember the birth of Jesus, that we may share in the song of the angels, the gladness of the shepherds, and the wisdom of the wise men.

Close the door of hate and open the door of love all over the world. Let kindness come with every gift and good desires with every greeting. Deliver us from evil by the blessing which Christ brings and teach us to be merry with clean hearts.

May the Christmas morning make us happy to be Your children and the Christmas evening bring us to our beds with grateful thoughts, forgiving and forgiven, for Jesus' sake.
Amen.

—ROBERT LOUIS STEVENSON

CHRISTMAS IS JOY & PEACE

❋

And there were shepherds living out in the fields nearby, keeping watch over their flocks at night. An angel of the Lord appeared to them, and the glory of the Lord shone around them, and they were terrified. But the angel said to them, "Do not be afraid. I bring you good news of great joy that will be for all the people. Today in the town of David a Savior has been born to you; he is Christ the Lord."

—LUKE 2:8–11

Good news from heaven the angels bring,

Glad tidings to the earth they sing;

To us this day a child is given,

To crown us with the joy of heaven.

—MARTIN LUTHER

Good Christian Men, Rejoice

Good Christian men, rejoice
With heart, and soul, and voice;
Now ye hear of endless bliss: Joy! Joy!
Jesus Christ was born for this!
He hath opened the heav'nly door,
And man is blessed ever more.
Christ was born for this!
Christ was born for this!

—J. M. NEALE

Joy to the World!

Joy to the world! The Lord is come:
Let earth receive her King;
Let ev'ry heart prepare Him room
And heav'n and nature sing.

He rules the world with truth and grace,
And makes the nations prove
The glories of His righteousness,
And wonders of His love.

—ISAAC WATTS

O morning stars, together

Proclaim the holy birth,

And praises sing to God the King,

And peace to men on earth.

—PHILLIPS BROOKS

Tell Me the Story of Jesus

Tell me the story of Jesus,
Write on my heart every word;
Tell me the story most precious,
Sweetest that ever was heard.
Tell how the angels, in chorus,
Sang as they welcomed His birth,
"Glory to God in the highest!
Peace and good tiding to earth."

—FANNY J. CROSBY

CHRISTMAS IS FAITH

❉

THE WORD BECAME FLESH AND
made his dwelling among us. We
have seen his glory, the glory of the
One and Only, who came from the
Father, full of grace and truth.

—JOHN 1:14

What Child Is This?

What Child is this, Who, laid to rest,
on Mary's lap is sleeping?
Whom angels greet with anthems sweet,
while shepherds watch are keeping?
This, this is Christ, the King,
Whom shepherds guard and angels sing;
Haste, haste to bring Him laud,
the Babe, the Son of Mary.

I am wishing you this day a happy Christmas.
I would send you those gifts that are beyond price,
outlast time, and bridge all space.
I wish you all laughter and pure joy,
a merry heart and a clear conscience,
and love that thinks no evil,
is not easily provoked, and seeks not its own;
the fragrance of flowers,
the sweet associations of holly
and mistletoe and fir, the memory of deep woods,
of peaceful hills, and of the mantling snow,
which guards the sleep of all God's creatures.
I wish that the spirit of Christmastime
may draw you into companionship
with Him who giveth all.
Come let us adore Him.

—BISHOP REMINGTON

Jesus

Wonderful—He would be wonderful in what He would accomplish for the fallen human race.

Counselor—He would be our Guide through life, and our Advocate before the heavenly Father.

The Mighty God—He would be the God before whom every knee shall one day bow.

The Everlasting Father—He would be the God of eternity.

The Prince of Peace—He would be the One who would ultimately bring a true tranquillity among the nations.

—KENNETH W. OSBECK

He was born in an obscure village, the child of a peasant woman. He grew up in another obscure village where He worked in a carpentry shop until He was thirty. Then for three years He was an itinerant preacher.

He never had a family or owned a home. He never set foot inside a big city. He never traveled two hundred miles from the place He was born. He never wrote a book or held an office. He did none of the things that usually accompany greatness.

Twenty centuries have come and gone, and today He is the central figure for much of the human race. All the armies that ever marched and all of the navies that ever sailed and all the parliaments that ever sat and all the kings that ever reigned, put together, have not affected the lives of man upon this earth as powerfully as this...

One Solitary Life.

A Christmas Blessing

God grant you the light in Christmas,
which is faith;

the warmth of Christmas,
which is love;

the radiance of Christmas,
which is purity;

the righteousness of Christmas,
which is justice;

the belief in Christmas,
which is truth;

the all of Christmas,
which is Christ.

—WILDA ENGLISH